Unmerited Favor

Raymond & Pamela Hicks

ISBN: 979-8-9878587-4-5

Disclaimer

This book is designed to share the author's life experiences and revelations. The author does not claim that the experiences and decisions shared within the book are ones the reader will experience or have experienced. The information shared within this book highlights a few difficulties and drawbacks that the author experienced and how he overcame them. Sound efforts have been made to ensure content accuracy. This book has not been written to condemn, point fingers, or target anyone. As a result, you agree never to sue or hold the author liable for any claims or similarities arising from the information contained within this book. Any likenesses to actual persons, alive or deceased, or personal experiences are merely to share the journey through the author's eyes. You agree to be bound by this disclaimer.

Dedication

We dedicate this book to all the men, women, and couples with issues. To those who cannot see the grace and mercy God has granted them over the years, this book is for you. It does not contain miracles or "Oh, my gosh" moments. It is simply us acknowledging God, the wonderful things He has done, and what He can do for you.

Raymond & Pamela Hicks

WHAT'S INSIDE

Acknowledgments

Pam and I would like to thank everyone who has entered our lives and supported us during the many times of disarray and turmoil.

We want to give special thanks to Debbie Hazley for her support and encouragement and for being a good friend when we needed her to be.

Thanks to Chameka Harrington for her honesty and for being a great daughter.

Thank you to our dear friend and photographer, Ray Sanderland, for the countless photos and memories, particularly our cover photo.

Last but not least, we give thanks, honor, and praise to our Lord and Savior, Jesus Christ.

Foreword

Raymond and Pamela Hicks are an inspiring and encouraging couple. Their life is a true example of the great and mighty things God can and will do in our lives if we trust and believe in Him. We all understand that we have disappointments, struggles, unforeseen situations, brokenness, good days, bad days, blessings, joys, and sorrows. But the Bible is very clear in 1 Thessalonians 5:16-18, in all things give thanks.

I have witnessed their family relationship get closer and stronger simply because they are living lives honoring Jesus Christ. I have witnessed the lives of their children and grandchildren being blessed because of the example they exemplify. Their book Unmerited Favor speaks on all those situations. It is an actual testimony of their lives, and it will take you on a journey to inspire, encourage, and bring joy to the readers, knowing that God is faithful. Praise God for His faithfulness to those who love Him.

Debbie Hazley

When asked by my parents to write this foreword, I was shocked but honored that they would ask me to be involved in their first book. Writing a foreword is not an easy task; it is the first part of a book where you, as the reader, decide if you want to flip the page or not. After you read this, I hope you choose to read this beautifully written book cover to cover and share it with a friend or loved one.

Let's begin. My name is Chameka Harrington. I have two children, Mashelle and Malachi, and I currently serve in the United States Air Force. As mentioned above, the authors are my parents. That (in itself) says a lot, as I have a daily front-row seat to see how God shows up for my parents. Raymond and Pamela's story will show why God's unmerited favor in their lives was worthy of praise.

As you journey through this book, I encourage you to write notes, highlight certain pages, start a book club, and even share your thoughts about the book with others. The authors are well-versed in this topic. I have witnessed firsthand how their lives have intertwined and how God has given them chance after chance. He continues to show them He is in control and that no man/woman can tear apart what God has placed together. Without giving you too much information before you read the book (because I assure you, you will want to keep reading it), do you remember the old saying, "How you get the man/woman could be the same way you lose the man/woman?" This book will show their relationship's ups and downs, trials, and tribulations. You may cry, laugh, shout, and maybe find yourself in their shoes, experiencing your testimony. This book was written with love and God's unmerited favor. It was an assignment placed in their hands, and they both executed it well.

Lastly, you may wonder why they would have their daughter write a foreword. It could be biased. It is not. My thoughts and opinions are my own. The authors are (indeed) the most qualified individuals to write this book as this is the story of their lives. And who is better to write an honest and accurate story about yourself than the people who have lived the story? You cannot falsify God's work and what He has done in your life. All information is backed up with facts, which is one of the many things that sets this book apart from others. Get ready to share in the Unmerited Favor in the lives of Raymond and Pamela Hicks!

Chameka Harrington

Introduction

As we mature in life, we begin to set goals for ourselves. As early as high school, we say, "Man, I cannot wait to get out of school," only to find ourselves in a new chapter of our life called adulthood. Some experiences can alter our lives for better or worse as adults. Our goals range from choosing to pursue a college education, entering the military, learning a trade, and, the big ones, getting married and having a family. But none of us have a crystal ball to predict what that will look like or what will happen. In life, we must step up to the plate and take a swing, even if what is thrown at us is a curve ball. Sometimes, you may hit a home run. On other swings, you may strike out.

Marriage is one of those curve balls. In fact, life is a learning curve. You see, God will never reveal his plans to you. If he had, we would not have known how to handle all the disasters, missteps, and unfortunate circumstances in our lives. Marriage is one of the biggest accomplishments we can attain (in our opinion). It is the most fulfilling, but it is a full-time job. Marriage is work. However, sustaining a marriage is undoubtedly one of the hardest things to do. Yet, it is not too hard for God. You must always stay inside his perimeter because one wrong step brings trouble. There are many barriers, obstacles, ups and downs, temptations, divisive measures, and self-centered behavior encompassing us that marriage seems to become overrated and downplayed. So much so that no one wants to get married. The one true and proven way to sustain a marriage is to stay true to what the bible says and believe God's word. What God has joined together, let no man put asunder. Life is difficult, but it can become overwhelming when you throw in marriage. When people get married, most do it out of infatuation, lust, desperation, or desire. Not often is love involved, and fewer people marry because of God. If you seek God and trust and believe in him, he will send the one true love that is right for you so that your marriage will be "until death does us part."

Unmerited Favor was written to help others understand the power of God and that he still performs miracles no matter how big or small. We also want our readers to discover how to recognize the grace he has extended to us. It is about two people who experienced some hard times throughout their marriage and how, with the help of the Holy Spirit, they managed to stay the course, knowing that God was with them. When you read this book, we would like you to focus on the power of God and not the situations we encountered. You can believe in God's ability to carry you through any situation. You may know someone in a similar position, or maybe it is you who is experiencing problems in life. Be encouraged. When you keep God amid your everyday activities, you can experience God's good plans for your life. Lean not to your (own) understanding, but trust that God is working things out in your favor. God is bigger than any life problem and only wants the best for his people. God takes care of his own!

Our book will take you on a journey of God's Unmerited Favor on our lives, how we made it through life's curves and survived to enjoy His grace and love. What God has for you is for you.

The Beginning

Hi, my name is Raymond. The beginning of my story may not be any different from most of yours. I grew up wanting to have fun like all the other kids. In high school, I had my share of girlfriends, played sports, got in trouble, skipped school, smoked, and sold marijuana (commonly known as weed). Yet, I managed to obtain good grades. Because of my grades, some thought I was a bit of a nerd.

Right after high school, in 1980, I joined the military—the United States Marine Corps. Ooh Rah! Yes, I became a part of the toughest, most elite military branch. In 1973, the United States was coming out of the Vietnam War, which officially ended in 1975. I was not thinking about that war or whether we would enter another conflict. I joined because I wanted to escape my hometown for a while. You know, get away, see the world, and, of course, serve my country. Man! The Marines had the sharpest uniforms. They called them "dress blues." Wearing that uniform provides a sense of pride and dignity. I was proud to have joined that branch, but some people thought I was crazy for joining. They asked, "The Marine Corps, why them? You know they are some crazy SOBs." I smiled and said, "Yeah, I know." As it turned out, we entered another conflict in 1983. The United States Embassy and Marine Corps Barracks in Beirut, Lebanon, were bombed. I was only three years in and thought, "Ok, here we go; another war was about to start, and I would be thrown into it. That was just the beginning. Eventually came the Gulf Wars and Operation Desert Storm. I was never sent into either conflict through God's grace and mercy.

Unmerited Favor

I served in the Marine Corps for 12 years before leaving in 1992. My time in the Marine Corps taught me a lot about myself. I found out just how much mental anguish I could take from someone, as well as my pain tolerance. But most importantly, I learned discipline, integrity, accountability, respect for others, self-respect, honesty, loyalty, trust, confidence, and commitment. All the characteristic traits one would need to survive in our unbelievable world. There was pride in knowing that I belonged to a brotherhood that promoted camaraderie, and when the going gets tough, those guys would have my back. Some people today, including my family, think I am what is known as a "shot-out." Shot-out is an affectionally used term for crazy because of the Marines. I blame it on my discipline and low tolerance for nonsense and stupidity.

In 1983, I got married. This was one of those instances where marriage was a desire and not total love. I thought I would be heading to Lebanon, and I wanted the girl I was dating to be my wife and protected financially if anything happened to me. Our marriage lasted for about ten years and ended in divorce. It was not all bad, though; we produced two beautiful girls. Our marriage ended because the love was not there anymore. It is not that we argued, fussed, and fought, but because the relationship was absolved of its love. Once she found out I might be getting deployed, she was set on returning home. All she wanted to do was go home and be with her family. Remember, we were just married, and she thought I would be leaving her to fight in a war. It did not change anything when we realized I would not be getting deployed. Her mind was made up. Although I did not deploy, much time was spent in the field training for what could still be a deployment. Due to the field training that comes with deployment, she always went home while I was training. Field training could last anywhere from two weeks up to three months. But even when I was home, she still wanted to go home. Ultimately, (I believe) that is the real reason our marriage did not survive. She was not one to live a military life.

Now, my life story begins. Sometime between 1992 and 1993, I met my - not knowingly - future wife. My brother, Tyrese, and his (then) girlfriend, Shaunda, were hosting a small gathering at his apartment. I was invited. When I walked in, I saw this petite, beautiful young lady that I initially thought was a little girl going to get a beer. I asked Pam (I learned her name), who are you getting that beer for, your mother? Pam looked at me with this arrogant attitude and said, "Naw! This is for me. This my beer." I then walked over to my brother, and I asked Tyrese, "What the heck are you doing with this little girl in here and allowing her to drink beer?" He looked at me dumbfounded as if I were a fool.

Well, things were beginning to kick into high gear. We were drinking, laughing, playing cards, and having fun. As is commonly said, one thing led to another. I started a conversation with the girl I thought was too young and discovered she was 22 years old and of legal drinking age. I was 29. She was this high-energy, bubbly little thing I thought I would like to get to know better. As the night aged and we got a little more intoxicated, things got a little more gratifying to us. This brings me to my first point of God's grace and his unmerited favor on me. I was in a rocky marriage with a wife of eight years at that time. I sought a way out since my marriage was on shaky grounds anyway. I knew what I was about to do was not right, but I did not care.

Unmerited Favor

God has a way of fixing things of which you are unaware. Now, don't get me wrong, I am not saying that God put his stamp of approval on my infidelity. But He allowed this to happen, and besides (in my opinion), mine was not a marriage approved by God either. No one knows how or when he does it, but He does. God provides his grace and mercy to us by extending unmerited favor. So, what is unmerited favor (you ask)? Unmerited favor is receiving an award, or reward for something you do not deserve. Webster defines it as "not adequately earned or deserved." Merit, on the other hand, is 1a, "a praiseworthy quality," 1b, "character or conduct deserving reward honor or esteem," and 1c, "a person's qualities, actions, etc., regarded as indicating what the person deserves to receive." Yes, I was married and about to commit adultery (cheat) with a younger lady I barely knew. I did not know the bible or God, for that matter, so I did not think I was doing anything wrong.

We started seeing more and more of each other, sneaking around with her, trying to keep her near me while not tipping my hand about my infidelity. I was bold. I got my then-wife to know her, and she also started to like Pam. Pam was even invited to our house to celebrate her youngest daughter's birthday. No one knew what was happening between us, but some suspected wrongdoing, including my momma. You know how those mothers are. They know their children and when things are not right with them. She had even asked me at one point if anything was going on between Pam and me, and of course, I denied there was. But God knew. Yet, he granted me grace and his unmerited favor. I did not deserve a second chance, but because God is a God of many chances, He knew I would make good on his word, Matthew 19:6, the second time.

Two years later, in 1995, that same young lady from the small gathering at Tyrese's apartment became my wife. In hindsight, I do not think God placed me and my first wife together. We married young, in another state, in a courthouse without any family around to witness our marriage, and for all the wrong reasons.

Here comes unmerited favor #1.

"Wherefore there are no more twain, but one flesh. What therefore God has joined together, let not man put asunder. Matthew 19:6. (King James Version)

When you know who God is and understand his love for you, you can then recognize all the wonderful things He does in your life. I truly believe God placed us together because we needed each other.

As I stated initially, my story may be similar to most of yours. Some of you may be thinking, I have never been married and cheated on my wife, or God would disapprove of such things. But some things in our lives were turned around for the good, and you do not know how it happened. Just believe it was God. The difference is how I came to know the Father, Son, and Holy Spirit, with an ability to recognize how and when I received His grace and mercy. Most of us do not recognize how much grace we have been given. We tend to think that everything we do is on our own. But God orders our steps every single day. The very fact that you were able to wake up this morning is all because of God. In essence, God allows some things to take place in our lives to show that we are not in control.

Unmerited Favor

We always want to blame the devil when things do not go right, but sometimes it is God allowing obstacles to exist to let us know HE is the great I Am and that his grace is sufficient. Here is the case and point. In late 2019, the world was introduced to a worldwide pandemic called COVID-19. It killed hundreds of thousands of people worldwide. All the people around the world thought the world was coming to an end; every nation wanted to blame China for spreading the virus, and politicians were trying to play God with the lives of the nation. Questions arose, such as who should or should not be vaccinated and how to stop the spread of this virus. But God, who is always in control, allowed this to occur to let the people of the world know that He is STILL God and in complete control of every situation. Four years later, in 2023, although the pandemic is over, the virus still exists, and for those of us who survived, we should thank God for his grace, mercy, and unmerited favor on us.

"then the Lord will overwhelm you and your children with indescribable plagues. These plagues will be intense and without relief, making you miserable and unbearably sick."

Deuteronomy 28:59 (New Living Translation)

"The Lord will afflict you with every sickness and plague there is, even those not mentioned in this Book of Instruction, until you are destroyed."
Deuteronomy 28:61 (New Living Translation)

The Beginning

There are countless ways that God grants us favor, and the bible is full of them. As you read your bible, you will begin to understand what was said and what is meant in the scriptures and how they apply to our everyday life. These scriptures were written well over two thousand years ago, yet they impact our lives today. Think back over your life and see if you can recognize any unmerited favors God has placed in your life. Then, give him thanks. I am not sure how many of you have heard what the acronym B-I-B-L-E stands for, but if you have not heard it, here it is again for those who have. Basic Instructions Before Leaving Earth. It is a guide as to how you should live your life.

The Facade

By 2000, we were in our fifth year of marriage, and things were pretty good. I re-enlisted in the Army National Guard after a ten-year hiatus so that I could retire. I only needed eight more years before retirement, and the National Guard would be the best way to achieve this goal. Well, at least that is what I thought.

While in the National Guard, I encountered several injuries that prevented me from sticking to my retirement plans. I could only complete six of those eight years of retirement before I was medically retired. I did not know that being medically retired and not finishing 20 years of service made me ineligible for retirement pay until I reached 60. I was only 43, but God had other plans for me. I was able to receive disability pay for my injuries to help accommodate and supplement my income until I reached my 60th birthday. By waiting on the Lord, he will take care of all your needs. Our plans are not his plans, and the Father knows best.

"but they that wait upon the LORD shall renew their strength; they shall mount up with wings as eagles; they shall run, and not be weary; and they shall walk, and not faint."

Isaiah 40:31 (King James Version)

Once I left the Marine Corps, I decided to invest in my community and give back my time by becoming a youth football coach. My tenure started in 1992. By 2000, I had experienced eight years of coaching, giving (my) time to my community and inspiring our youth to be better and more productive citizens rather than just football players. I was good at it, too. Our team put in work around the city helping clean up parks, picking up trash along the roadside, and holding car washes to help raise money for items not furnished by the organization, such as duffle bags in which to carry their uniforms, team t-shirts, food for after the games, and more. I earned Coach of the Year honors in 1993, numerous city championships, Offensive Coach of the Year in 1997, and Defensive Coach of the Year in 2002. My teams experienced eleven playoff appearances and won seven championships during my tenure. I coached four different organizations throughout sixteen seasons.

Here is a look at my typical workday. At 4:30 am, I would get up and get ready for work. By 6:00 am, I am at work until about 4:30 pm. A typical 10-hour workday for me, five days a week, was not unusual. My schedule allowed me plenty of time to get home and relax before heading out to the field for practice, which started at 6:00 pm and ended around 8:30 pm. By the time I got home from practice, it was well after 10:00 p.m. on most nights. That was before the actual season began. Once the season started, we practiced only three days a week due to school for the kids. Sixteen weeks of practice, games, and playoffs make for long days, especially after you have worked all day.

On game day, which was Saturday, I arrived at noon and remained at the field until 10:00 pm or later. Once the games were over, our coaching staff talked, evaluated the game, and made game plans for the next week. Youth football around these parts was taken seriously. There were bragging rights involved, city rivals, coaches getting to know other teams' coaches and their coaching styles, comradery with your organization, and not to mention "The Championship Trophy" at the end of the season.

We would typically feed the kids after every game unless it were an away game. Following all of that – every week – it was the coach's time. Beer, liquor, cigarettes, weed, and cocaine were always part of our Saturday post-game meetings. I never used cocaine on the weekdays, during or after practice. I only engaged with cocaine on the weekends. I was what one would call a "functional cokehead." I did not smoke weed at all because the THC stayed in the body system too long, and I knew I had to go to work the next day. I had a really good job that subjected me to random drug testing at any given time. But that was not on my mind when I indulged in that activity, but I was still conscious of my intake so as not to indulge too much because of my job. I thought I had a surefire way to beat any drug test at any given time. Imagine this. I never tested positive for drugs.

Here comes – at a minimum - unmerited favor numbers 2 -7. All those random drug tests and not once a positive result? That was all God. In my naivety, I thought it was all me passing those drug tests on my own. But God was working on my behalf. Did I deserve it? No! I cannot recall the countless number of times I wondered if this would be the drug test that would send me packing and back home to my wife to explain that I got fired due to a failed drug test. That would have devastated her. She had no idea what I was doing. She thought I was going to football practice and hanging out with the fellows, not indulging in cocaine and other recreational activities. I was to her, her knight in shining armor and the one who was supposed to provide for the family. Getting fired would not have been a good look. I give God thanks for delivering me from that lifestyle.

"When you follow the desires of your sinful nature, the results are very clear: sexual immorality, impurity, lustful pleasures, idolatry, sorcery, hostility, quarreling, jealousy, outbursts of anger, selfish ambition, dissension, division, envy, drunkenness, wild parties, and other sins like these. Let me tell you again, as I have before, that anyone living that sort of life will not inherit the Kingdom of God."
Galatians 5:19-21(New Living Translation)

Now, let's return to this story's real meat and potatoes. Throughout my five-year marriage, I was unaware of the impact that staying out all day and night and on Saturdays was having on my wife. I was not a choir boy then, but I never cheated on my current wife. Yet, I was living a lie, a façade, a double life. My life as a husband with a good job was different from my football coach and drug life.   No one knew both sides except my coaching buddies – AND GOD.

Things started to change. I did not think of it much then because she seemed all right with me going to practice. She did her thing, and I did mine. Work, football practice, late nights, home, repeat. I never knew her routine because I was never there. Then, I noticed that Pam (my wife) arrived home after 9:00 pm on the nights I had practice. I did not think much of it then, but it was a sign of things to come. I should have paid more attention to the signs. Pam was not wearing her wedding ring.

She was gone when I was gone. Ironically, these were some of the same things I did when I cheated on my first wife. However, it hit differently. It was happening to me. My wife and I were drifting apart.

God is truly a wonderful and amazing God. Just when it seems to be the darkest of times and things start to unravel, He will step in and make it right. God's mercy and grace are what brought us through those times. We were both doing wrong. As we now know, God is a healer, and he forgives us of all our sins. We must have faith, and God sees our faith when no one else can.

Meet my wife, Pam, as she shares her story.

Daddy's Girls

Hi, my name is Pam. I am Ray's wife. As a little girl growing up in a house with sibling brothers, I longed for a sister. My brothers had each other. I admired their bond, but it made me feel I lacked something. I always wanted a little sister, someone I could play with and talk to about anything. I was it: me and my baby dolls. I would go outside with my friends, and we would roller skate, cheer, play jacks, hula hoop, and run around. We were kids. As a kid, I had better not let the streetlights come on while I was still outside. Momma did not play that. We had to be in before dark! Anyway, my momma did not have any more children, so I had no choice but to grow a bond with my two brothers, whom I admire for looking after me and teaching me the ropes. I love them.

I spent quite a bit of time with my dad. Whenever he left the house to go to the bar and shoot pool, he took me along. Yep, little old me, hanging out with my dad, sitting on the other pool table as he shot pool and won! My dad did not want to leave me home with my brothers because I was "his little girl." Doing so was his way of protecting me. Of course, my brothers would not let anything happen to me, but my dad just wanted to be sure that his daughter would be safe. He would get so mad at the guys in the bar for cussing around me, but they would tell him, "Well, you know you shouldn't bring her in here." Even though I was young, I always felt safe and protected when I was with my dad. I knew he would never let anything happen to me in that bar. He knew momma would put him in a headlock if anything happened to me. She did not play about me. I was her only daughter. So, he was very attentive to me and my surroundings while I was there. Can you believe it? No matter how often I went with my dad and watched him and those guys shoot pool, I never learned how to play or shoot pool. My brothers learned the skill, but not me. You would have thought I could play after spending all that time at the pool hall.

My dad was the best. Men would pay him when he won. Afterward, we would drive up 4th Street back home. But before we arrived home, I always got what I wanted: a bag of Doritos (red bag) and a pickle. That was my reward for hanging out with him. My mom was always looking for her ONLY daughter to arrive back home. When we came home, I was happy to see my mom, and she was so glad to see me, too. But as for my brothers, they were jealous because I had snacks. Although it was fun to watch him play, I still had no one to talk to and share how my dad beat those men at a game of pool and acquired all their money. I would stay in my room talking to my imaginary friend and baby dolls. Occasionally, I played outside in the park with a few friends.

One day, my mom told me that I had a sister. Just like that, out of the blue, she states something that I had always longed to have. Where did she (my sister) come from? I had many questions. But for the moment, I left it alone. All I wanted to do was meet my sister. Days, weeks, and months went by, and I anxiously awaited to meet my sister. I could not wait to meet her. I did not consider her "our" sister. She was "my" sister. I was glad to have one. When the day arrived for us to meet my sister my brothers and I rose early to take the ride with Dad to the Greyhound bus station to pick her up. The ride to the Greyhound station seemed long, but it was short. I wondered why Mom did not ride with us, but in the 1980s, children knew not to ask or question parents about WHY!

While heading to the station, all kinds of thoughts came to my mind. How did she look? Was her hair nappy like mine? What color was her skin? Was she tall, short, fat, skinny, or what? I wondered if she was mixed (bi-racial). Guess what? She was bi-racial. She was the most beautiful, caramel-skinned little girl I had ever seen as she exited the bus. The way I acted, one would have thought I had won tickets to Disney World. I was very excited and could not wait to get to know her. She was happy to meet us, too.

Tamara. Wow! How cool that her name rhymes with mine. Ta-ma-ra and Pa-me-la. I loved that. We had a few things in common besides our names. Once we began talking to each other, we realized we were Daddy's girls. That was the happiest day of my life. I finally met my new sister. I was so happy. She had the prettiest, smooth hair. I could not wait to play in her hair. After returning home, I took her to meet some of my friends. We had so much fun together, laughing and playing games. I taught my sister to play jacks, braid hair, and cheer. You know, all those things little girls do. We stayed up late every night to spend as much time together as possible. We spent so much time talking and trying to get caught up in our lives that we didn't get much sleep. My brothers also spent some time with our new sissy. They told jokes that were not (really) funny, but we laughed at them anyway. However, they did not introduce Tamara to any of their friends. They did not want any of their friends hanging out over at our house or trying to get to know her. I guess they figured someone would try to "holla" at her, and my brothers did not want any of their friends talking to their sister or me. All I could think was that I finally got a sister. The reunion did not last long. Tamara only stayed for a week before returning home to her mother. I did not see her for nearly the whole remainder of that summer. Yet, I anxiously awaited her next visit.

Sometimes, I prayed my sister would come back and (even) move in with us. However, I knew it would not happen, yet I kept praying. My friends asked when my sister would return to visit, and I would always say, "Soon."

Many years passed by without seeing each other. I lost my virginity at 16 years old, conceived, and gave birth to my first child at 17 years old. It was this very moment in my life when I broke my daddy's heart. Becoming a mother at a young age left a bitter taste in his mouth. His "baby girl" became pregnant and a mother. He was not happy at all. His dissatisfaction caused me to consider having an abortion.

My dad was beyond disappointed. He was angry. After all, I was still one of daddy's girls. The next time I saw my sister, I was living alone with my first daughter. My sister, Tam, finally made it back down to see us. During her visit, we took the bus to the mall, took pictures, ate at the food court, met up with friends, and shopped. Tamara was so happy to be with me, her big sister. I loved playing the role of hairstylist. I told Tamara I would like to do her hair in a style because it was so soft and curly. She probably was tired of me playing in her hair, but she never said anything.

As we both grew older and I got married, our relationship faded. When my dad heard that I was about to get married, he was unhappy. Even though my future husband, Raymond, did come and talk to him and ask for his blessing, he said he was not planning on attending the wedding. My dad loved me, and I loved him too, but he thought he was losing his daughter. Instead, he was gaining a great son-in-law. In the end, he did attend the wedding.

Tamara and I remained in contact and saw each other occasionally on the weekends. When Tamara married, our relationship dwindled even more.

"Wives, submit yourselves unto your own husbands, as unto the Lord. For the husband is the head of the wife, even as Christ is the head of the church: and he is the savior of the body. Therefore, as the church is subject unto Christ, so let the wives be to their own husbands in everything. Husbands, love your wives, even as Christ also loved the church, and gave himself for it;"

"So ought men to love their wives as their own bodies. He that loveth his wife loveth himself."

Ephesians 5:22-25, 28 (King James Version)

Yet, despite the paths our lives took, we never lost our love for each other. Since we lived only a few hours away, we would arrange trips to spend time with each other. There were times when Ray and I would take our mini-vacations, weekend stays, or staycations, as we like to call them, in Orlando, where my sister and her husband lived. We would always let them know we were in the area, and they would visit us at the resort. We would meet on one of those weekend days and go to dinner or return to their house to talk and catch up on life. Life has its way of taking over at times, but we know God is still in control, and God knows best!

Looking at your life and seeing everything you have gone through, you could ask yourself, "Man, how did I get through all that? I got a three-letter word for you. G-O-D. I do not know where I would be right now if it were not for the Lord on my side. Even as a little girl growing up, He had me in mind. He watched over me through my teen years, during my pregnancy, and in my adult years as I married.

"He will cover you with his feathers. He will shelter you with his wings. His faithful promises are your armor and protection. Psalms 91:4 (New Living Translation)

"The Lord keeps you from all harm and watches over your life. "The Lord keeps watch over you as you come and go, both now and forever. Psalms 121:7-8 (New Living Translation)

Can You Say Promiscuous?

My coming-of-age story climaxed when I became sexually active. My pregnancy was by accident. I was not intending to have a child at such an immature age, but it happened. I was taught about contraceptives and how to protect myself sexually, but I chose not to listen. I was naïve in thinking a pregnancy could not happen to me. Back then, teen pregnancy was not as prevalent as it is now. I was 16 years old and still living at my parent's house. When I got pregnant again, I had to move out of the house and get my (own) place. Even though I was incredibly young, I had to trust that God would carry me through all this. One thing I love about my God is that he will never bring you to something without getting you through it. The tests and trials we experience can be used to testify to his goodness. Furthermore, the mess we find ourselves in always has a message. God has his way of doing things, and for that reason and many more, I love him. I had two more kids, and I am proud to have them.

Nonetheless, the physical satisfaction of intercourse was new and exciting to me. During those moments, my worries were gone. The feeling was so enticing that it became addictive. I spiraled into a girly-girl, sinful world where the devil just would not let go. I was what one would call promiscuous and (very) sexually active.

"Don't you realize that your body is the temple of the Holy Spirit, who lives in you and was given to you by God? You do not belong to yourself, for God bought you with a high price. So you

21

must honor God with your body.
1 Corinthians 6:19-20 (New Living Translation)

The first physical touch from a man catapulted me into a satisfaction-seeking cycle, resulting in the birth of four beautiful children: three girls and one boy. Yes, I was happy to have a son! Our family's fertility rate proved to be extremely high. You could spell the word s-p-e-r-m and get pregnant. Sex was not my only issue. However, sex was my way of coping with the loneliness of being young and on my own. I thought being out on my own was me being an adult, but the reality is that I still had a lot to learn. I had so much to deal with and a child to care for. My youthful eyes witnessed a lot of wrongs, and my deeds fell right in line with the mischief. I was stealing, lying, skipping school, smoking weed, and drinking, which I detest all together today. I was in and out of relationships, unable to stay still or with one man. When the devil knows the wrong you are doing, he will do whatever it takes to keep you there. It's like he (just) had his way with me. My misdeeds led me down one wrong path and into one big mess after another. I laid back and did things by myself, even got in trouble by myself, all while moving from place to place.

Since my sister was not in the picture for me to confide in or hang out with, I finally decided to chill and revisit my options as a young lady, settling into a new apartment with four children whom I do not regret entering my life. I got serious about my job, work habits, school, and who I hung around with. Then I met Shamy. Shamy was this beautiful, light-skinned lady who lived on the same street as me. She was very nice to me, and we eventually began spending a lot of time together. She would even watch my kids while I went to work. My brother stayed with me during this time, but not for long. He eventually moved out into his place. At some point, while he was there, he saw I was being a girl player. He would tell me that I needed to stop, but I ignored his negative comments and advice at that time. So, I kept doing things I thought brought happiness into my life. This included heading to my friend's house to have fun. My brother advised me not to go. Again, I dismissed his advice.

That ole' devil never stops working. When things start looking up, he comes rearing his ugly head again. He was trying to keep me from going to my friend's house by whispering nonsense in my head. The devil was working through my brother to get to me. He will go through your family if he can't get to you. I thought I was delusional. I began hearing voices, or so I thought. It was God telling me everything was going to be okay. God alone was speaking to me, not my brother. My brother was trying to protect me from myself, and I loved him for his concern. But God. He knew what was about to happen. He knew there was someone out there for me. God allows things to happen on purpose, so in the end, he gets the glory because you will realize he kept you. Let me tell you how I met my husband of (now) 28 years.

That night, I met this guy at my friend's house. He and his girlfriend were having a party. The brother (of the guy I met there) was my neighbor, and I was good friends with his girlfriend. They were having a card party and invited me over. I was excited to leave the house and have fun with people I felt would not land me in trouble. We were having a great time. Eventually, I laid eyes on a light-skinned guy. Let me be clear. I was not a fan of light-skinned men. I liked my men in a dark chocolate hue. Although he regarded me as a little girl (I later learned), all it took was a little reassurance from his brother and his girlfriend that I was "as grown as they come." We sparked a conversation. Our conversation led to fornication for me and adultery for him. I did not care. I was already spiritually dead. Oblivious to who I was as a person, I merely reduced myself to an ugly woman with four children to raise, who turned to sex to get what she wanted.

I believed no one wanted to help me raise my children and be with me, but I was wrong. Eventually, this guy and I grew to love each other so boldly that our affair came to light. He, too, had a family with two girls but soon got divorced. I was not trying to break up his marriage, but he told me that since he was not happy, he was about to get a divorce. I was glad to hear that and wanted to be with him. He accepted my 4-pack, and we married and became a blended family.   I call this Unmerited Favor because neither one of us deserved what God had granted us – each other.

God is a God of many chances. Although we may think we do not deserve His grace and mercy, He provides it anyway. When things do not go right in life, do not give up. Do not think it is hopeless. Because God, in all his infinite ways and wisdom, knows what is best for you – and me - in life.

"You say, "Food was made for the stomach, and the stomach for food." (This is true, though someday God will do away with both of them.) But you can't say that our bodies were made for sexual immorality. They were made for the Lord, and the Lord cares about our bodies. 1 Corinthians 6:13 (New Living Translation)

If moments cause you regret or pain, take them to the Lord in prayer. Ask Him to help you see those moments not through your own eyes but through His. God's grace through his son Jesus sets us free from our sins. This is why he died for us. When trouble comes your way, and you begin to doubt yourself, pray. Pray for forgiveness and protection over yourself. Reflect on your past afflictions and failures and see how God can turn you away from the temptations while leading you down a path of righteousness. He did it for me, and He will do it for you.

Love or War?

Here we go. Let's rewind a bit. Our marriage was in turmoil. We could not stand the sight of each other. We were yelling and cursing at each other for no good reason. In fact, we searched for a reason to argue. On some days, she would snap for no good reason, and on other days, it would be me. Then, the sex started to dissipate. We went from sexual intercourse two to three times a week to once a week to once a month to almost none. She even stopped wearing her wedding ring. Why did I not see the signs? Remember, I was married before. These are some of the same things I did when I went outside my marriage to my first wife. All I knew was that this was my second and last marriage, and if it did not work out, I was done.

So, why was our marriage taking such an abrupt turn? I knew I was not stepping out, just hanging out. But what about her? Was she feeling unwanted because of my late nights and weekends? This pattern of turmoil and uncertainty lasted for several years in our marriage. If anyone has ever experienced an on-again, off-again kind of marriage or relationship, this was it. I love you today, but not tomorrow. Do not say or do anything to piss me off kind of marriage – yes, this was it.

We tried to get along during it all, and when we did, it was great. We attempted to rekindle our marriage with date nights and doing the things we thought were satisfying to us, like smoking weed and drinking. But that was not enough. Our marriage went from bad to worse. We needed God. The drugs and alcohol were of no help.

As we were sitting in the house watching TV, the phone rang. We had an onscreen caller ID, so the TV displayed the caller. I asked Pam if she was going to answer the phone. She looked at me and said, "No, you answer it." So, I did. Without hesitation, the guy on the other end had the nerve and audacity to ask to speak to her. This dude was bold; he spoke confidently as if my wife was his, and I was just some guy on the other end of the phone. One thing led to another, and the conversation worsened. The dude began to describe the inside of my house. At that point, I thought I was going to lose it. But I remained as cool and calm as I could. My wife was sitting there right beside me, hearing the entire conversation. After ending the conversation, I was not sad, mad, angry, broken-hearted, or anything. Surprisingly, my heart was in a forgiving mood. I knew our marriage was in trouble, and if I went in on her about the conversation that just took place, it would only make the situation worse. She would have shut down and felt threatened, and no conversation would have occurred. I was not yelling or cursing at her but I wanted to know who he was, their relationship level, where they met, and most importantly, why she had found interest in another man. That was the day everything came to light. She had already discovered I was using cocaine.

One day, my brother and a few friends were at the house. We sat in the backyard on the patio, talking and shooting the breeze. Pam was in the kitchen washing dishes. She peeked out of the window and saw what we were doing. I pretended I did not see her looking out the window and kept doing what we were doing. She never said anything until the day of the phone call when, simultaneously, I found out she was having an affair. An affair that was so bold that she even had her boyfriend come to my house when I was not home. MY HOUSE!

Pam and I had a brief conversation about the affair, and she finally asked if I was using cocaine. I could not lie to her, knowing that she already knew, and doing so would make matters worse. All I could think of (at the time) was another failed marriage. I was adamant. If this marriage did not work out, it would be my last one. I knew something or someone had to change in this relationship if it would work. But it didn't. Not at that time.

Our relationship progressed to the point of violence. I put my hands on her, not physically hitting her but forcefully grabbing her and pinning her up against the wall on several occasions. There was an incident where I ended up in jail for the weekend. We got into a big argument; I threatened her, she called the police, and I spent the weekend in jail. I was issued a restraining order and could not return to my house. The house I bought using my VA benefits. How did we get there? What happened in our relationship? Was this love or war?

When Pam left, I thought our marriage was over.

"I said to myself, "I will watch what I do and not sin in what I say. I will hold my tongue when the ungodly are around me." But as I stood there in silence—not even speaking of good things—the turmoil within me grew worse. The more I thought about it, the hotter I got, igniting a fire of words:
Psalms 39:1-3 (New Living Translation)

As a woman, I knew this was not what I signed up for. Thus, with all the chaos and dysfunction, I decided to move out. I did not want to be married to someone who yelled all the time and was abusive. So, while he was at work, I slowly moved some of my clothes out of our closet so he would not notice. We had a big closet with his and hers sides. Thus, I knew he would not notice a few things missing. It only took me a week to completely move out.

When Ray came from work, I was gone, living in an apartment with my youngest daughter and grandchild. To help me out, the guy I was seeing had paid for my apartment. Ray was unaware of our new location. He called me wanting to talk, but I would not answer. When I did answer the phone, I was rude and mean to him. He did not need to know where we were staying because I did not want him visiting me. Somehow, he discovered the address and showed up uninvited. I could tell he had been drinking. I still cared for him and his safety, so I allowed him to stay overnight to sleep it off. The next day, we said our goodbyes. Yet, for me, I felt as if he could keep it moving. I convinced myself that I would do life alone, live independently, and not have to answer anyone anymore. Plus, I could come and go as I pleased. I danced around acting as if I was happy, but in reality, I was lonely. I missed the home-cooked meals, bills being paid, getting spoiled, and having extra money for shopping. You name it, Ray did it. I cannot deny that Ray was a provider, but I detested being under any man's authority. I felt like marriage was not for me, and maybe I had rushed into this marriage. I should have gotten to know Ray better before rushing into a marriage with him. I wanted to be called Mrs. Hicks so bad that I did not realize what

I was getting into, and at what price. I kept saying, "This is not what I signed up for."

My flesh kept telling me, "You are good." So, I continued to dismiss the signs from God. I knew Ray was a good man, but I did not want to believe he or I could change. So, I went back to the days of being on my own before I met him. I started to hang out with old friends again. I spent much of my time drinking and clubbing and avoided going to work as much as possible. Being out all night made getting up and going to work hard, so I would call off. I did not like to cook, so being in the kitchen did not sit well with me either. Ray did all the cooking. I cooked a small meal occasionally, but for the most part, if it was up to me, we ate out. I did not even know how to change the oil in my car, not to mention the act of paying for my car note. Ugh! Ray did all that.

A month later, my car was repossessed while I slept at home. The vehicle was purchased from one of those buy-here, pay-here dealerships where payments were due bi-weekly. They would come for your car if more than two payments were missed. I wanted some things from the store, so I went shopping. I had spent the car note on some outfits and other things for me, my daughter, and my grandson. Yet, my flesh kept telling me I was good. Although things started looking bad, I refused to return to reality. I got an eviction notice once again and still refused not to go home. I moved in with a friend. I kept running. Sin had me captured longer than I wanted to be. It seemed as if a leach was sucking the life out of me and would not let go. Yet, I kept ignoring the voices. Some friends and loved ones would advise me to return home and give God a try, to not give up on my marriage, but Nah, I'm good.   But I was not good. I was a ticking time bomb about to blow.

"Therefore judge nothing before the time, until the Lord come who both will bring to light the hidden things of darkness and will make manifest the counsels of the hearts: and then shall every man have praise of God."
1 Corinthians 4:5 King James Version

It's Now or Never

When I decided to leave, live life, and start my journey in my girly girl world, I believed I could do what I wanted and not be pressured by any MAN or his authority! My husband's actions caused me to be very blunt and open about how I lived. I did many wrong and not-so-pleasant things while I was out there. Some call it living your best life! I had low standards and low self-esteem. While hurting inside, something would tug at me or whisper, saying, "Go home." Well, my flesh told me I was already home. Nonetheless, I could not deny it. I was lonely, unhappy, weak, and needed direction. That whispering voice in my ear was none other than the voice of God.

"Then I realized that my heart was bitter, and I was all torn up inside. I was so foolish and ignorant—I must have seemed like a senseless animal to you. Yet I still belong to you; you hold my right hand. You guide me with your counsel, leading me to a glorious destiny. Whom have I in heaven but you? I desire you more than anything on earth. My health may fail, and my spirit may grow weak, but God remains the strength of my heart; he is mine forever.

Psalms 73: 21-26 New Living Translation

When the devil has you under his wing, it is hard to recognize the connection you have to God's power. My ways had caused turmoil in our family. I was confused and hurt by my actions. My inner self showed up and controlled my being. I did not care who I hurt and what I was doing, so I kept doing it. The fleshly takeover further immersed me in a world of sin until God said, "Enough! You are better than this. Come to me, and I will give you rest, my child." I heard him, but I kept running and doing whatever I wanted. I moved from place to place, enduring one eviction after another. I lied and stole from Peter to pay Paul (as is commonly known when there is not enough money to cover all expenses). I was doing what some call "the most." The fact that I never became addicted to using drugs remains a point of pride amid my mess. What I was addicted to was the wrong type of FREEDOM. See, God did set us free from the bondage of sin, but for some reason, I kept my freedom connected to sin.

"Have mercy on me, O God, because of your unfailing love. Because of your great compassion, blot out the stain of my sins. Wash me clean from my guilt. Purify me from my sin. For I recognize my rebellion; it haunts me day and night. Against you, and you alone, have I sinned; I have done what is evil in your sight. You will be proved right in what you say, and your judgment against me is just."
Psalms 51:1-4 New Living Translation

I had to dig deep and search for what I (really) needed. Temptation approached daily. I did not know God was still trying to reach out to me. He stood across from me, extending his loving hands while waiting for me to grab them. I was so blind. I could not see Him. I was deaf and could not hear Him. Sin's guilty stains had built up within me, and I felt like my lungs were clogged. My disgust was likened to a toilet being backed up, requiring it to be cleansed, needing a plunger to release the toxins, and finally getting the mess out. I needed a change, and that change was on the horizon. I began to hear my Pastor say, "You are a new creation; all things have passed, and behold, old things are new." Was this for me? God does use people to get his message across to the intended recipient.

Things began to turn around when I stopped fighting my inner spirit. I will never forget my conversation with my Pastor's wife, whom we affectionately call "First Lady." Her words came forth in vivid illumination. Yet my flesh was still unwilling. She continued to speak to me, encouraging me. She would say, "Give God a try." As she spoke, I could sense my spirit as willing, but my flesh was not. I was stuck on a fence with my feet dangling above the ground.

Once she left, I took her advice (in part). I lost my job, and my bills became (even) harder to pay. Another eviction notice arrived, and I had nowhere else to go. Men viewed me as a single woman. My life tasted as bitter as black coffee and looked like black coffee, too—pitch black, void of light. Finally, I did what the Holy Spirit told me: "GO BACK HOME!" I went.

There I was, settled at home, but not out of the darkness and in the clear. The devil still had me sneaking around and holding back instead of being 100% honest. I was confused about my decision and struggled to submit to my husband. There I was, at home, vulnerable, lost, wounded, and sinfully scarred. Ray welcomed me back home with open arms. I was unsure if he had changed, but I trusted God and wanted to believe him when he said he had changed. My husband brought to my attention that I frequently wore black clothing and was distanced from our relationship. He pointed out that those were signs of depression. Unaware of the signs of depression I was displaying and the fact that I had already rejected the notion and willingness to submit to my husband, I definitely did not want to listen to him, let alone listen to him talk about the type of clothes I wore and my mental state.

I could not shake it. I felt out of place and very confused. Temptation was always present. I tried disconnecting from it, but it seemed like it would not go away. My husband still did not trust me completely. Whenever I approached the door, he would say, "Are you going to see your boyfriend?" My flesh wanted to lash out (verbally) at him, but I could not do it. All I could say was, "If you do not trust me, let me leave because I refuse to keep listening to you remind me of what I have done. It is bad enough that my parents are disappointed in me." I needed healing, not scolding. Every time they spoke, it was like diarrhea of the mouth. Nothing but shit was coming out. Some days, I would sit and cry. I disconnected from my family and did not want to touch my husband or have sex with him. Just let me be, I thought. I was still in a hurt place. I (just) needed a loving hand, a voice, a smile, a kiss on the forehead that said it would be okay. But nope. The sinful views kept coming up over and over until God came and wiped my tears away and said, "Get up and sin no more; you have been forgiven."

It was tough to be intimate with my husband, knowing what I had done and was doing with another man. Yet, there was a turning point. I stopped running from God and admitted that I needed help. I needed a cleansing. My turning point arrived after

I began attending church faithfully. I still wavered. Even while attending church, I tried to convince myself that church was not where I wanted to be. The Holy Spirit remained present and told me to keep fighting for what was right and not what I liked. I knew it had to be now or never. God gave me a choice - his side or the devil's side. God convinced me that his side is much better, cleaner, brighter, and more peaceful. Come to me, and I will give you rest, my daughter.

After joining the church in 2014, I remember sitting in the back, trying to be discreet. A beautiful young usher came over and hugged me. She said, "It will be okay." I thought, dang, she knows, too. So, I wanted to run out of there, but I remained and rocked my grandson to sleep. My husband was sitting a few rows ahead. I did not want to sit next to him because of the shame. It seemed as if the whole church knew my business. It seemed as if people were looking all around at me. HELLO! Can you all stop it and pay attention to what's happening in the service? OMG! Church folks. I now realize it was the devil trying to make me paranoid. No one was looking at me. The people were nice. It was me tripping because of the shame. I love my church family, but I could not imagine going through this. I felt like Jesus was punishing me for what I had done.

My Mom would say, "Jesus loves you, and we do too. Go back home to your husband and stop hurting yourself (and Ray). Please try Jesus, baby." My life was like a tug-of-war. Yet, our God won the fight. I gave it a try and went back home.

"In the same way, you wives must accept the authority of your husbands. Then, even if some refuse to obey the Good News, your godly lives will speak to them without any words. They will be won over by observing your pure and reverent lives."
1 Peter 3:1 New Living Translation

Three-Year Hiatus

For three years, 2010 – 2013, we were separated. Yet, I was still in love with Pam. When she left, I was extremely hurt. I tried everything I could to win her back. I constantly called her, made time to meet up with her, spent nights at her place, and chased her all over the city, trying to win her back. I knew something or someone had to change in our relationship if it would work. So, I started to pray more, talk to God, ask for forgiveness, and change my ungodly ways. I asked him to bring my wife back home to me.

As I attempted to win her back, the thought of her being with her boyfriend (or whomever) occasionally came to mind. It seemed to happen so quickly. The emotions I did not or could not feel while she was talking to her boyfriend that day began manifesting. I destroyed everything in our home that reminded me of her. I took all the pictures off the wall, packed her remaining clothes, placed them in a bag, and put them in one of the other bedrooms, thinking this would prevent my mind from thinking of her. I even did the worst thing imaginable. I burned all our wedding pictures. Yes, I burned the entire album. I was trying to process all this and make sense of it. Why was this happening to us? I thought God hated me for doing what we did. The affair with her, the fornication, the drugs, all of it was coming back on me.

Although we were still married, I had no one to hold on to. I needed love, too. What did I do? Of course, I turned to another woman for affection, but it was a short-lived relationship that only lasted a few months. I was so in love with Pam that I could not be with another woman, so my focus returned to winning her back. I had to do something, and God told me exactly what I had to do.

"Come to him", he said. "Put your trust in me, and I will give you rest." At this point, I had nothing else left to try except God. During our three years apart, I did not know God was preparing me for something bigger. There was a transformation about to take place in my life that I was not expecting. God allows things to happen in our lives to make us aware of him. When things do not go right for us, the first thing we do is call on Jesus. We say things like, "Jesus, please help me." "Oh God, if you get me out of this, I promise I won't do it again." "Oh God, take this pain away." Whatever the problem, we always call on God. No matter if we believe in him or not. But there has to be some belief, or else you would not call on him, right? I have never heard anyone say, "Satan, please help me."

When I bought my house in 1992, I thought it would be the home I would have forever. I had been living there for nearly 15 years, and I had no idea I was about to lose it. (at least, I thought so). I got to a point where I did not care what happened to the house. One day, I met up with an old army buddy. As we talked, he asked me to come to his church. I replied, "Your church?" He said, "Yeah, my church. I am the Pastor of a church. Come by and check it out." I told him I would visit.

Months passed. I never stopped by or attended. I was still in my head, thinking I could get by without God. My army buddy kept reaching out for me to attend; I kept promising but never showed up. Then, one day, I gave in. I attended a service and enjoyed it. I was no stranger to church or God. However, I did not KNOW GOD.

Things were getting bad. Darkness before the storm had arrived. I was at a crossroads. I wanted my wife back; I was about to lose my house, and I did not know how to deal with either issue. So, I just stopped. I stopped everything, prayed more, and attended church regularly. By this time, I had not paid my mortgage for two years. I wondered what the heck was going on. No mortgage payment was sent for two years, no foreclosure notice, no letter from the bank, or even a phone call. I mean, NOTHING! In the meantime, I enjoyed attending church while discovering who God was and his love for his people. I did not worry about the house or what could happen to it. Getting to know God was more important to me than the house, and that was just the beginning.

"Trust in the Lord with all your heart and lean not on your own understanding; in all your ways submit to him, and he will make your paths straight.
Proverbs 3:5-6 New International Version

Several more months passed, and I still had yet to pay my mortgage. The day arrived when I finally received a letter. The letter advised that I must appear in court regarding my mortgage. When I went to court, I did not know what to expect. But I knew enough that this matter must be placed in God's hands. I asked the Lord to do whatever was necessary to deliver me out of this situation. At the hearing, the judge asked me why I had not paid my monthly mortgage payment and what I planned to do about the delinquency. I replied, "Your honor, I am not interested in keeping the house. They can do with it what they want because I cannot afford to pay the amount owed." The judge then looked at the mortgage loan officer and said, "You heard him. Do what you need to do." I walked out of that courtroom feeling so relieved. I felt good. You must be wondering why I was so happy about losing my home. I was unhappy about losing my house but ecstatic about how God's word is always true. I was not worried. It has been said that we should pray and not worry, but if you are going to worry, then do not pray.

"Therefore, I tell you, do not worry about your life, what you will eat or drink; or about your body, what you will wear. Is life not more than food, and the body more than clothes? Look at the birds of the air; they do not sow or reap or store away in barns, and yet your heavenly Father feeds them. Are you not much more valuable than they? Can any one of you by worrying add a single hour to your life? And why do you worry about clothes? See how the flowers of the field grow. They do not labor or spin. Yet I tell you that not even Solomon in all his splendor was dressed like one of these. If that is how God clothes the grass of the field, which is here today and tomorrow is thrown into the fire, will he not much more clothe you—you of little faith? So do not worry, saying, 'What shall we eat?' or 'What shall we drink?' or 'What shall we wear?' For the pagans run after all these things, and your heavenly Father knows that you need them. But seek first his kingdom and his righteousness, and all these things will be given to you as well. Therefore, do not worry about tomorrow, for tomorrow will worry about itself. Each day has enough trouble of its own.

Mathew 6:25-34 New International Version

Convinced that God was still working in my favor, two more years passed, and my wife was back in the house. I explained that we may have to move soon, and the house is approaching foreclosure. It had been five years since the mortgage company received my payments. Miraculously, I received a letter from the mortgage company stating that all my payments were current and I owed nothing. What? Thank you, Jesus. Won't he do it? We later decided to downsize and decided to sell the house.

Our marriage was looking good, and we were feeling good. We were in a wonderful place in our lives. God changed our way of life. He delivered me from the drugs, changed my mentality, brought forgiveness in my heart, returned my wife home, and opened Pam's eyes to see His goodness and what He can do when you trust in him and have faith.

Redemption

One Sunday in 2013, I sat in church, holding our grandson as the service closed. The doors of the church were opened. This means an invitation was extended to join the church and give my life to Christ. It felt like someone was pulling me by the shirt and dragging me up to the front to the altar to give my life (back) to God. Once I reached the altar, the pastor asked, "Is there anything I wanted to say." I announced out loud, "I want my marriage to work." Then, I looked into the congregation and saw this beautiful woman smiling back at me. She had a pleased look on her face. It was the First Lady. My faith was elevated when my Pastor gave me a great big hug. I thanked God for what he had done. At that moment, I was on cloud nine. I was high – on God. Lol.

I completed the church's New Members Orientation over eight weeks. It was just the beginning of God preparing me for my calling. When I got to know God and what he wanted from me in return, I got heavily involved in church. I joined the choir and usher board, worked as the Pastor's secretary, became a Deaconess, and started teaching New Members Orientation. Was everything good? Nope. The devil was still after me because he knew that I was on the verge of being free from sin and his grip. I was still vulnerable and very much ashamed. There were some good and not-so-good days at church, and my dang on flesh was still very weak, but my spirit was stronger and more willing. The Holy Spirit kept saying, "I LOVE YOU PAM. Let it go, and let me in." God said I will put no more on you than you can bear. Give it to me. The more I became involved in church, the more I grew and learned. However, I still was not out of darkness nor in the clear. The toxic thinking kept showing up, making me think I made a big mistake. I thought I was fooling myself. I would say, "Faith, destroy the doubt and fear in me, and give me a clean heart." As my faith got stronger, I reminded myself that I was forgiven.

Fast forward. It's 2016. My wife and I are back together, and God was still working on us. Our marital relationship had improved drastically. We stopped arguing and began enjoying being in each other's presence. If you have forgotten, this book is about God's unmerited favor and the grace he has extended to me and my wife. As our relationship with God grew, he continued to bless us with the little things in life. We were blessed with the things most of us take for granted, such as peace of mind, health, finances, and faith.

By this time, I had been at my job for 18 years—no more smoking cigarettes, cocaine, or weed. I drank only on rare occasions. I never tested positive for drugs. My mortgage was paid off. My wife realized the error of her ways, joined the church, and began getting to know God. I rededicated my life to Christ and actively served as a Deacon in the church. Yeah, you guessed it. I joined the church my Army buddy asked me to attend years ago. Yes, the one at which he was the Pastor.

I later took on the roles of Usher Board President, Pastor's Aid Vice President, Media/Sound Technician, and Sunday School Teacher. It seemed our marriage was going through a very deep, detailed car wash. Life was looking good. The more time we spent with other believers and in God's word, the more God became visible. Our relationship started to get (back) on track for the better. We restored date nights to our schedule, went on trips, walked on the beach, communicated better, prayed together, and even discussed how messed up our relationship was in the past—no marriage counselor. No therapist. Just God. We were being redeemed. Our redemption was brought with a price. A price that Jesus paid for us all. Our broken fences were being mended.

Our story is much like that of Ruth. We do not see miracles or divine intervention from Heaven. We see God subtly at work as He guides the two women down a path of restoration and fruitfulness. When we face challenging times, we must not rely on human understanding or take the easy way out. Instead, we must seek God for His purposes. Not only did our poor decisions negatively affect Pam and me, but they also affected our family as a whole. Are we perfect? No, we are not. But God sees our flaws and knows our paths. This is why there is redemption.

"In him, we have redemption through his blood, the forgiveness of sins, in accordance with the riches of God's grace."

Ephesians 1:7 New International Version (NIV)

"for all have sinned and fall short of the glory of God,

and all are justified freely by his grace through the redemption that came by Christ Jesus."

Romans 3:23-24 New International Version(NIV)

As time passed, God continued to bless us. I managed to stay on my job for 27 years before retiring. I did not know what God had planned for us when I left that job. I walked away from that job, expecting to find greener pastures.

I began working for an insurance company. It was a commission-based job. If I did not sell any policies, I would have no income. There was no other source of income other than my wife's income and my retirement pension. When I told Pam I was leaving my current job to sell life insurance, I sensed she was unhappy about my decision. However, she stuck with me as I encouraged her that everything would be all right. God had everything under control. We were able to witness more of God's unmerited favor.

With her income being our primary source along with my retirement pension, we managed to keep a roof over our heads, keep the utilities on, and cover all our other bills while (still) being able to enjoy somewhat of a social life. Did all the bills get paid on time every month? No! But they did get paid, and service was never disconnected. That's faith, that's favor, that's God.

We had two cars that were on their last legs. One was a 2007 Ford 500, and the other was a 2015 Nissan Altima. I decided to trade in the 2015 Nissan Altima for something newer. Even with no real source of steady income, I knew we needed reliable transportation. With the confidence that God would provide for us, I asked Pam if she wanted a new car. Of course, her answer was a resounding "heck yeah!" We proceeded to the car dealership because we walked by faith, not by sight.

Redemption

"Jesus answered and said unto them, Verily I say unto you, If ye have faith, and doubt not, ye shall not only do this which is done to the fig tree, but also if ye shall say unto this mountain, Be thou removed, and be thou cast into the sea; it shall be done."
Matthew 21:21 King James Version

Once at the dealership, we went through the usual process of viewing different cars. However, I knew what kind of car I wanted for Pam. We were about to sign the paperwork, and the salesperson asked if I was also interested in getting a car. I told her, "Only if we can get a two-for-one deal." She said, "Well, let's look at a few." I finally settled on a 2018 Nissan Titan truck, and Pam was getting a brand new 2021 Nissan Rogue with only six miles on the dash. I thought, man, ain't God good? But that was not the end of the deal. The sales manager said, "What if I can get you into a brand new 2021 Titan for the same price as this used 2018?" Not thinking the deal would go through anyway, I sarcastically asked what the color of the 2021 model was. Pam said, "It's gotta be blue. That is his favorite color." The manager said, "I am unsure what color it is because it just arrived." So, he had them drive the vehicle to the front. Lo' and behold, it was a 2021 BLUE Nissan Titan with a paint color named – get this - Ray G blue. WOW! That day, we drove off the lot with two vehicles for the trade-in value of our one 2015 vehicle. Both vehicles were brand spanking new. But wait, that still was not the end of God's favor. The finance rates were 0%. Can you say unmerited favor and grace? We could not have expected anything more.

More grace came into our lives over the years. We opened a gospel hip-hop social club. The club or event center was designed for Christians to go and enjoy praise and worship with live music, praise dancers, poets, and gospel rappers. People of all ages were welcome to join the festivities and host social events and gatherings. The club did not last long, but we are so grateful that God allowed us to experience it as a business and worship his name in that manner. No worries. We will restart our club soon.

"Let them praise his name with dancing and make music to him with timbrel and harp.
Psalms 149:3 New International Version

Even though I was technically unemployed, I could still generate a source of income by being self-employed. Pam started several small businesses that were good sources of extra income, such as a Paparazzi Consultant and a customized crafts business. Her crafts were handmade, including glitter wine glasses, Liby print glasses, military plaques, pens, children's composition notebooks, and more. Pam managed her businesses while working full-time at a hospital. God says that if you put your trust and faith in him, your gifts will make room for you.

"Bring ye all the tithes into the storehouse, that there may be meat in mine house, and prove me now herewith, saith the LORD of hosts, if I will not open you the windows of heaven, and

pour you out a blessing, that there shall not be room enough to receive it.   Malachi 3:10 King James Version

Restored

When my husband left his job, I was discouraged by the thought that I may have to hold down the fort. Little did I know God had other plans for us.

I prayed while trusting God to keep us on the path he had chosen for us. Also, I wanted an understanding of where our lives were heading. Eventually, another job opportunity became available, which paid me more than I (initially) earned. I went for it. I thought this was the right thing to do since Ray leaving his job made me very uneasy. When things start to look good in life, that old devil sure has a way of showing up. He will tempt you with things, but all that glitters ain't gold. Unfortunately, I did not have faith in God as I should have had. My husband kept encouraging me that everything would be all right, but I would not listen. The grass is not always greener on the other side.

After accepting the new job, I put in a two-week notice at my job, which I had been on for nine years. The new job allowed me to work from home, and the company provided all the equipment needed.

My first day on the job went well. Yet, I discovered that the company's structure differed significantly from what I was accustomed to. As time passed, my happiness turned into sadness. This job was not for me. I could not work in an environment with strict rules and demands. It lasted two weeks, and I decided to quit.

I texted my old manager at my previous job inquiring if my (old) position was posted. To my surprise, he was very excited to hear from me again. He stated that he had just submitted it and advised me to go online and reapply for the position. Once I submitted my application, he retrieved it, reviewed it, and I was rehired. But God.

The managers at my previous job were happy about my return. My tenure and benefits continued right where I left off since I was gone for less than a month. I received notification from the Human Resources Department that a merit increase had been implemented across the board. Guess what? I was entitled to the merit increase in addition to my annual increase, which placed my income above that of the job I thought was right. I received above and beyond anything I could have ever asked for. God was (and is) the bomb. The lesson here is that God wants us to wait for his increase in our lives. However, we often get in the way. I told God I would not move anymore until he told me to. I have been at my current job for ten years and received recognition after recognition. I was given more responsibility to assist the managers with new employee training. In the meantime, my business started to pick up, and my creative side became more evident. Through my work, God showed me that I was more than just a face in this world.

As my wife began to experience success in her job and as a business owner, I was given more opportunities for testimonies. God can get your attention even when you are not paying attention. Over 15 years ago, I was diagnosed with diabetes. I did not think much about it and treated it like any other medical diagnosis. I did not know the actual severity of it and the effect it can have on your life. I did not know the symptoms, how to treat them, or what signs to look for. So, I just continued living my life as if nothing was wrong. Diabetes is not called a silent killer for nothing. When they sang that song that says I could have been dead, sleeping in my grave, well, I should have been dead, sleeping in my grave. But for God's grace and mercy, it could have been me.

One Friday, while sitting at home, I began to get dehydrated and a bit lightheaded. No matter how much water I drank, I could not quench my thirst or overcome the lightheadedness. My wife kept telling me to go to the doctor, but I kept telling her I had an appointment on Tuesday. I drank gallons and gallons of water. Pills for dizziness did not help either. Sunday arrived. While in church, sitting on the front pew with all the deacons, my pastor was watching and observing everyone. He noticed me and how I looked. After the service, he asked if I was okay. I told him I was fine, and he said, "You don't look fine." My wife told him what was going on, and he instructed her to take me to the hospital immediately. I, being stubborn, told her not to take me to the hospital and that I could wait until Tuesday for my scheduled appointment. Of course, she took me anyway, and thank God she did.

When I arrived, the doctors assessed all my vitals, checked my blood glucose level, and reported an astonishing 750 BG reading. The doctors wanted to know how I was still alive and how did I walk into the hospital. They were surprised I did not go into a diabetic coma. Nobody but God. So, they pumped me with insulin, and my body went into complete rejection, locking up like I had a giant muscle cramp. Every part of my body tightened to the point that I could not move. I stayed in the hospital for three days, recovering. God was not through with me yet and I am so grateful. I still have diabetes, but now I know how to manage it. God can get your attention when He needs to, even when you are not listening. He is in the blessing and healing business. You must let him in.

I said I wanted to share a couple of testimonies, and here is the second one. This testimony occurred at work. There are people in this world who, no matter what you do or who you are, will not like you. We tend to call those people racist, but God loves us all regardless of our flaws. And when you are under the covering of God, he will always keep you safe from liars, cheaters, backstabbers, and those who do not have your best interest in mind or want to do you harm. I had recently been transferred to a new work section. I was the only black person in the section. I had yet to gain experience in this section, nor was I familiar with the product they serviced. Let me be clear: I was a third-level test technician and could test and troubleshoot with the best of them. However, being unfamiliar with a product, there is still training that needs to take place. When I asked for help, they responded, "You're a third-level tech. Figure it out." This group of employees was hell-bent on not showing me what they did and how to do it. It was left up to me to figure it out on my own. Well, after several failed units and the threat of being written up if the problems persisted, I was inclined to report the entire section to HR as racist. We ended up having a group session to discuss the issues in the group, how to improve the working conditions, and how to get me the proper training. However, what came out of the session was that I was still getting written up for accusing the group of racism. To my surprise, HR did not want to know that they had racist employees in their midst. Proverbs 3:5-6 KJV says, "Trust in the

LORD with all thine heart; And lean not unto thine own understanding. In all thy ways acknowledge him, and he shall direct your paths." I was dumbfounded and floored that they took that approach toward me for reporting what I perceived as racist employees. After our group meeting, I was scheduled to speak with an HR representative again. I was advised that they were not going to write me up. That should have never happened anyway. However, three weeks later, I was transferred to another group. This is how God works in your favor when you are under his anointing. Three months later, that entire department was shut down; two employees were laid off, one retired, and the other two were sent to two different departments to work. Additionally, the HR representative was fired. To this day, I still do not know what happened and who intervened, but I do know God was in the midst of it all. I went on to serve 27 years with that company and retired.

We thought God was done with us, but He was not. God continued to bless us in more profound ways than we could imagine. He blessed Pam by allowing her to co-author her first book, Girl Pick Up Your Crown. Then, he elevated both of us to on-screen status with parts in a movie, Daddy, U Misspelled Father, which airs on Tubi TV.

Waiting on God requires discipline because waiting can be discouraging at times. When wanting something so bad that you are willing to do whatever it takes to get it, it means you are not waiting and trusting God to see you through. He will work it out when you give it to the Lord. This battle is not yours; it's the Lords. So, pray to the Lord and watch him move things. That is why reading your bible and getting to know him is important.

As time passed, Pam and I learned more new things about each other. God takes us all through a growing process. We must grow and evolve to co-exist.

Ray is my MacGyver. There is nothing he cannot do. Ray will get it done. If there is a way to fix or rig it to make it work, he will do it. He is a great handyman. He enjoys reading, writing, and teaching. Ray is the kind of person you would want in your corner. He will have your back if you are right and tell you when you are wrong. If you do not have a MacGyver, you better find one. No degree is necessary. Only God.

Pam is my rock and my voice of reasoning. She will set me straight when necessary. She always knows the right thing to say to calm me down. Even when I pretend not to hear what she is saying, her words still get through. She is an understanding and kind person who will do whatever she can for others. Pam always thinks more of others than herself. That is God. She has a special gift of being a "people person" with a very loving personality. No degree is necessary—just God.

Are we done? I don't think so. Do we still have issues and experience not-so-good days? Without a doubt. That is life. God never carries any of us through life to leave us. He never said life would be easy. There will be trials, tribulations, ups and downs, and good and bad days. However, when we face challenges in our lives now, we know how to handle them better, and that is by praying and seeking God for his help and guidance. God is not done with us yet. We know He has bigger plans for us because God is bigger than life.

We pray that you enjoyed reading our book and discovered something to help you recognize God's unmerited favor in your life. We are not marriage counselors, nor are we ministers or pastors. We are two ordinary people who found out how to survive because of God and with His unmerited favor. May you be inspired, encouraged, and, more importantly, become in tune with God. We did not write this book to preach to you but to let everyone know that God is real. He can change your life if you trust him, have faith in him, seek him, and give your life to Him.

THE END

10 Tips for a Lasting Marriage

There is no (real) way or solid answer to making a marriage last. We can only speak about what we did to make our marriage last for 28 years and counting. Our way is not the only way, but it was and is our way. Put your (own) spin on some of these principles and watch God work. However, make no mistake. If God is not a priority in your marriage, all else is superficial.

Tip #1

This may sound corny to some, but it worked for us. Whatever you did to get that man or woman, keep doing it. Something attracted you to each other. Maybe it was your smile, swagger, mannerisms, body, or personality. Whatever it was, please do not stop doing it. You owe it to each other to maintain or rekindle the spark between you. We understand that as people grow, their bodies and personalities change. I am not the same twenty-nine-year-old stud I was when we first met, but my body has not gotten obesely out of shape. We have grown more mentally than physically.

Tip #2

Date nights are a must for all couples. It is always good to spend time with your spouse. In our society nowadays, nobody has time for anything but work. Working to the point of exhaustion does not leave time for each other. Do not make excuses for not hanging out with the woman or man of your dreams. After all, they are the ones you said, "till death do us part." Date nights allow for time to get to know your spouse. We encourage you to set aside a minimum of one or two nights a month for date night. Ideally, once a week is the goal. Do not forsake doing the little things. A walk in the park, a movie, bowling, dinner, or even a drive around the city or to another city has great value.

Tip #3

Take Vacations. Now we know some of you say, "Ain't nobody got no money or time to take vacations." NEWSFLASH. Your job can operate without you for a week or two or a weekend. You are not that important. Everybody is expendable because if they fire you today, your job will be posted within the hour and probably filled within a week. Vacationing does not necessarily mean big, expensive trips to exotic places. It can be a weekend trip to a new city in your state or a 4 – 6-hour drive to another nearby state. We like to call those types of trips STAYCATIONS. Staycations are close enough to home, but you will probably not spend much money. The result is that you spend quality time with your boo. Wherever you decide to go, make the best of it.

"I observed yet another example of something meaningless under the sun. This is the case of a man who is all alone, without a child or a brother, yet who works hard to gain as much wealth as he can. But then he asks himself, "Who am I working for? Why am I giving up so much pleasure now?" It is all so meaningless and depressing. Two people are better off than one, for they can help each other succeed. If one person falls, the other can reach out and help. But someone who falls alone is in real trouble. Likewise, two people lying close together can keep each other warm. But how can one be warm alone? A person

standing alone can be attacked and defeated, but two can stand back-to-back and conquer. Three are even better, for a triple-braided cord is not easily broken.
Ecclesiastes 4:7-12 New Living Translation

It is best to stop living according to man and start living according to God's will. Be happy with the one you are with.

Those first three pieces were all about spending time with each other while getting to know yourself and your spouse. The more time you spend together, the better you will understand, respect, and appreciate one another. The time spent together allows for a greater appreciation of when you are apart during girls' trips or boys' getaways. Remember, time spent apart is not a license to cheat. Everyone needs a little "me" time.

Tip #4

Treat each other with respect. One of the quickest ways to divorce is disrespect. Some say finances and cheating are the fastest ways to divorce, but you can fix those things. However, once you have lost respect for each other, arguments tend to ensue regularly. Neither person cares what the other one says, does, or thinks. It is all about self. The house is in disarray, tension builds on every front, communication is lost, and the joy is gone. Respect means allowing the man to be the man of the house and the woman to be the lady.

Ladies, do not try to be the man if you have a husband. His job is to provide for you and his family. The provision includes but is not limited to, a roof over your head and making sacrifices for the family when necessary, even if it means going without. Protection includes preventing hurt, harm, or danger - seen or unseen; keeping the family safe and caring for and defending the family. The man must promote, encourage, support, and discipline when necessary. Ladies, be a nurturer, teach, care for, help develop, be a help mate, aid, assist, and cultivate. When the two roles are mixed up, things get out of line and messy, and respect is lost.

"Submit to one another out of reverence for Christ. Wives, submit yourselves to your own husbands as you do to the Lord. For the husband is the head of the wife as Christ is the head of the church, his body, of which he is the Savior. Now as the church submits to Christ, so also wives should submit to their husbands in everything. Husbands, love your wives, just as Christ loved the church and gave himself up for her to make her holy, cleansing her by the washing with water through the word, and to present her to himself as a radiant church, without stain or wrinkle or any other blemish, but holy and blameless. In this same way, husbands ought to love their wives as their own bodies. He who loves his wife loves himself. After all, no one ever hated their own body, but they feed and care for their body, just as Christ does the church.

Ephesians 5:21-29 NIV (New International Version)

Tip #5

Communicate. Learn to talk to each other, not at each other. Never go to bed angry at one another. Life is too short to be mad at anyone, let alone all night. Listen to each other, and do not try to out-talk each other. No one is listening if you both are talking at the same time. Tell each other you LOVE them daily. Share your opinions, but do not be judgmental. Be supportive. It is okay to disagree. However, do not let disagreement cause you to have a bad day. You will be surprised at what you can learn from each other when you talk. Everything does not have to go your way. There is always a compromise in the conversation if only you listen to each other.

"Do not let any unwholesome talk come out of your mouths, but only what is helpful for building others up according to their needs, that it may benefit those who listen.

Ephesians 4:29 NIV (New International Version)

Tip #6

Trust each other. How can two walk together if they are divided? A house divided will not stand against itself.

"Any kingdom divided by civil war is doomed. A town or family splintered by feuding will fall apart. And if Satan is casting out Satan, he is divided and fighting against himself. His own kingdom will not survive."
Mathew 12: 25-26 King James Version

Trust must exist in your relationship. Judgment and not believing in each other spell disaster. Lying to circumvent the truth does not help with trust issues, either. Trust, as well as respect, is earned in a marriage. Do not give either person any reason to feel otherwise. Trust, Honor, Love, and Respect. WOW! Those powerful words can break or make a marriage, or any relationship, for that matter. Let your word be your word, and do not question the other because what is done in the dark will eventually come to the light.

Tip #7

Have fun, smile, be silly, and laugh together. All work and no play make Jack a dull boy. Nothing kills a marriage faster than boring people. It is okay to be "silly" sometimes in a marriage. Having fun is how we grow—together. Most of us do not want to be around our (own) family because we think they are boring. Thus, when a new family (with a spouse) is created, why look elsewhere when you have your lover, best friend, girlfriend/boyfriend, confidant, or supporting cast beside you 24/7? Do not let your marriage go stale.

Tip #8

Embrace change. As you grow, so will your relationship. Change is inevitable, and it is something we all must overcome. When you accept (good) changes in your spouse, be it their mindset, personality, physical appearance, or whatever, do not criticize them for changing. Embrace the change with a compliment. Do not be afraid to show your true feelings when necessary. Tough love is overrated, and it is NOT Godly. God is love. What he wants more than anything is for us to love each other.

"Love is patient, love is kind. It does not envy, it does not boast, it is not proud. It does not dishonor others, it is not self-seeking, it is not easily angered, it keeps no record of wrongs. Love does not delight in evil but rejoices with the truth. It always protects, always trusts, always hopes, always perseveres.

1 Corinthians 13:4-7 NIV (New International Version)

Tip #9

Be creative. Find new ways to enjoy each other. Do not be afraid to take your relationship to new heights. Learn what each other likes by exploring different sexual preferences. We are not discussing exploring relationships outside your marriage but more about "how to please" your spouse. Live life with great expectations. Be daring. Life is too short not to have fun.

Tip #10

Last but not least, SEEK GOD FIRST! In fact, God is the most important of the ten. Keeping God in the forefront of your marriage will get you through the most challenging parts of your marriage. When things seem hopeless, and there is no one else you can turn to, turn to God. He is your father when you are fatherless. He is your mother when you are motherless. He is a lawyer in the courtroom. He is a doctor in the operating room and a friend when you are friendless. God will never leave you nor forsake you. That is a promise. Ask, and you will receive; seek, and you shall find; knock, and the door will be opened. When you pray, pray with an expectation that it will be done. Be sincere when you pray. When you pray, understand that a delay does not mean denial. Why? Because God works in his own time and is always on time. He is not only the Father, Son, and Holy Ghost but also a lion, the lamb, and the G.O.A.T. He corrects and disciplines when necessary. He is gentle, shows compassion, and grants mercy when needed. He is the Greatest Of All Time. None can compare to who he is. God, Jesus, and the Holy Spirit is very much alive. You need to have faith. What is faith? Faith is the substance of things hoped for and the evidence of things not seen (Heb 11:1). We will leave you with this fact.

"For God so loved the world, that he gave his only begotten Son, that whosoever believeth in him should not perish, but have everlasting life. For God sent not his Son into the world to condemn the world; but that the world through him might be saved.

John 3:16-17 KJV (King James Version)

Our Favorite Bible Verses

These are a few of our favorite scriptures that help us remain encouraged and navigate life's challenges. As you experience any of these emotions, may these scriptures help you gain an understanding of God and his love for you.

Upset – John 14

Weak – Psalm 18:18-36

Lonely – Psalm 23

Sin – Psalm 51, Romans 3:23, and Psalm 51:4

Worried – Matthew 8:23-27

In Danger - Psalm 9 and Romans 8:31-39

Anxious – Philippians 4:4-9 and Matthew 6:25-34

Leaving on a Trip – Psalm 121

Lack of Faith – Exodus 14 and Hebrews 11

Depressed – Psalm 27, Psalm 34:18, and Matthew 11:28

Unhappy – Colossians 3:12-17 and Romans 7:25

Seeking Peace - Matthew 11:25-30, John 14:27, and Philippians 4:6-7

Need Courage – Joshua 1, Isaiah 41:10, and Deuteronomy 31:6

Need Direction – Psalm 73:21-26, Jeremiah 29:11-13, and Proverbs 3:5-6

Struggling with a Loss – Luke 15, Revelations 1:1-11, and Colossians 3:1-17

Struggling Financially – Psalm 37, Deuteronomy 28:12, and Proverbs 13:22

Discouraged with Work – Ecclesiastes 12: 14, Proverbs 10:4, Revelations 22:12, and 2 Thessalonians 3:10

Thank you for purchasing our book. We pray that it inspired you and provided a sense of belonging and acknowledgment that God is real and alive. Our book was not written to be a bible but to give glory to God for all He has done in our lives. We could not give him glory without referencing his word and how it applies to our everyday lives, yours included. There's nothing new under the sun. The Bible was written over two thousand years ago, and as you have read in our book, you can go to scripture for ANY problem in your life. If you enjoyed reading our book, please share it with others. Thank you, and God Bless.

About the Authors

Raymond Hicks was born in St. Petersburg, Florida, to Frederick M. Hicks Sr. and Peggy Ann Howard Hicks. Raymond attended and graduated from Boca Ciega High School, Gulfport, Florida, in 1980. Soon after, he enlisted in the US Marine Corps and served honorably from 1980-1992. In 2000, Raymond reenlisted in the Army National Guard and served until 2007. He retired due to medical reasons after serving 19 years of military service.

Raymond's educational accomplishments are:

- Associate of Arts degree from American InterContinental University in Business Management.
- Bachelor of Science in Business Administration Management.
- Master of Business Administration Operation Management; and
- Master of Science in Information Technology Project Management.

In 2015, Raymond was ordained as a Deacon and attends Mt Pilgram Missionary Baptist Church in St. Petersburg, Florida. He is also a member of the American Legion.

Raymond worked for GE Aviation from 1992 to 2019 as an Avionic Repair Technician, where he retired after 27 years of service. Raymond currently works for Jabil Defense Aero Space as a Solder Inspector.

Raymond has been married to his wife, Pamela, for 28 years. Pamela is a co-author of this book, Unmerited Favor. They have a blended family of six children, five girls and one son, with a combined 18 grandkids.

Raymond's favorite Bible verse is Philippians 4:13 KJV: "I can do all things through Christ, who strengtheneth me."

Pamela Hicks was born in St. Petersburg, Florida, to Eddie Lee Hawthorne Sr. and Mary Jane Hawthorne. Pamela attended Lakewood High School but received her GED from the YMCA in St. Petersburg, Florida, in 1990. After high school graduation, Pamela enrolled in Remington College, where she studied health courses and received medical certification as a medical assistant. From 1994 to 1996, Pamela worked as a medical assistant at Johnnie Ruth Clark Medical Center. In 1996, Pamela transferred her skills as a Medical Assistant to work at LeVine Surgical Medical Center as a Rectal Nurse.

From 2000 to 2004, Pamela ventured into the direct-selling industry by becoming a Mary Kay Independent Beauty Consultant and an Avon Consultant.

Pamela continued her education by obtaining her Associate of Arts in Business and Health Administration from American InterContinental University (AIU) in 2007.

Pamela worked as a Registrar 1 for St. Anthony's Hospital and a Phlebotomist for One Blood from 2010 to 2013. She is a Customer Service Rep II at Johns Hopkins All Children's Hospital.

In 2015, Pamela became a Deaconess and attends Mt. Pilgrim Missionary Baptist Church. Her service at Mt. Pilgrim once included singing in the choir. However, she serves on the Usher

Board, is the Pastor's secretary, and teaches New Members Orientation.

Pamela is a part-time entrepreneur with various businesses, including, but not limited to, being an Independent Paparazzi Consultant and crafter.

Pamela has been married to her husband, Raymond, for 28 years. Raymond is a co-author of this book, Unmerited Favor. You can find Pam's creations by going to www.pamsprettythings.bigcartel.com.

Pamela's favorite quote is "Safe, Sealed, and Secure." Her favorite Bible verse is Isaiah 41:10 NIV: "So do not fear, for I am with you; do not be dismayed, for I am your God. I will strengthen you and help you; I will uphold you with my righteous right hand."

Made in the USA
Columbia, SC
16 June 2024

37240197R00043